basic flavorings

Vinegar

basic flavorings
Vinegar

Clare Gordon-Smith

photography by

James Merrell

COURAGE
BOOKS
AN IMPRINT OF RUNNING PRESS
PHILADELPHIA • LONDON

Art Director **Jacqui Small**

Art Editor **Penny Stock**

Design Assistant **Mark Latter**

Editor **Elsa Petersen-Schepelern**

Photography **James Merrell**

Food Stylist **Clare Gordon-Smith**

Stylist **Sue Skeen**

Production Consultant **Vincent Smith**

Our thanks to Christine Walsh and Ian Bartlett.

© 1996 by Ryland Peters & Small

Produced by Mandarin Offset
Printed and bound in China

10 9 8 7 6 5 4 3 2 1
Digit on the right indicates the number of this printing

Library of Congress Cataloging-in-Publication number
96-67171

ISBN 1-56138-779-7

This edition published in the United States of America in 1996 by
Courage Books, an imprint of
Running Press Book Publishers
125 South Twenty-second Street
Philadelphia, Pennsylvania 19103-4399

Notes:
Ovens should be preheated to the
specified temperature. If using a
convection oven, adjust times and
temperature according to
manufacturer's instructions.

All pickles and preserves should be
processed in a boiling water-bath
canner according to USDA guidelines.

Vinegar is made from various alcoholic liquids, such as red and white wine, sherry, cider, malt, and rice wine. It occurs naturally when the liquid comes into contact with bacteria in the air, forming a surface film of yeast cells, which then convert the alcohol into acetic acid. This film is called the "vinegar mother," and can be removed and added to fresh supplies of liquid to produce more vinegar.

Aromatics may be added to vinegar (usually red or white wine vinegar), and the result used to flavor dishes or dressings. Fruits, herbs, and spices—such as the tarragon, rosemary, garlic and chiles, peppercorns, and bay leaves shown here— may be used to make flavored vinegars at home, provided the bottles and corks are sterilized before use. Keep these preparations in the refrigerator or a dark cupboard for two weeks to **infuse** the flavors, then use as soon as possible. Match each flavor to the principal ingredient in a dish to **enhance** the effect—for example, tarragon vinegar with chicken dishes, and orange vinegar with duck. When being used in cooked dishes, vinegar should always be reduced first, in order to burn off the acidity, leaving just the **essence** of the flavors behind.

the flavors of **Vinegar**

Because vinegar is
made from alcoholic
beverages, the vinegars produced
in each country reflect the drinking traditions
of those regions. From left, very old **sherry
vinegar**, rich and mellow, comes from Spain.
Light red **Chianti vinegar** is made from the
light, elegant, red wines of the Chianti region
of Tuscany,
Italy. **White
wine vinegar** is
made in most wine regions of the world,
including France, America, and Australia.
Japanese **rice vinegar** is based on their rice
wine, and is mild and complex in flavor. Light
and dark Chinese rice vinegars (not shown)

8 The flavors of vinegar

have
stronger flavors.
Red wine vinegar,
like white, is produced in
all the wine regions of the world. Its darker
color is the result of keeping the grape skins in
contact with the juice for a longer period.
Balsamic vinegar is the king of vinegars,
aged for up to 30 years in wooden casks. The
finest is from Modena in Northern Italy. Cider
is the basis of **cider vinegar**, used for pickles
or complementing other fruit flavors. Dark
malt vinegar, made from malted barley,
originates in Northern Europe, where beer is
the traditional drink. Its paler cousin, far right,
is used for pickling light-colored vegetables.

The flavors of vinegar **9**

Salads

Thai salad
with orange and sesame dressing

Thai food is known for its clean, fresh, zippy flavors, and this recipe is no exception. Fish sauce—sold in Asian markets as *nam pla*—together with rice vinegar are the definitive taste ingredients in this simple salad. Serve as a light-as-air appetizer, or with a selection of spicy dishes, noodles, and rice.

Slice the Belgian endive leaves in half lengthwise, then place in a bowl with the shiitake mushrooms. To make the dressing, heat the vinegar, ginger, sesame oil, garlic, and brown sugar in a saucepan, stirring until the sugar is dissolved. Pour over the mushrooms, add the orange juice and Thai fish sauce, then set aside to marinate for 1 hour. Blanch the sugar snap peas by plunging into a large saucepan of boiling salted water for 1 minute. Drain quickly, and refresh immediately in cold water. Drain again, then mix into the salad and serve.

1 head of Belgian endive, if available, or radicchio

8 oz. fresh shiitake mushrooms

8 oz. sugar snap peas

sesame dressing

½ cup rice vinegar

2 tablespoons pickled ginger (see page 58)

2 teaspoons sesame oil

1 garlic clove, crushed

2 teaspoons brown sugar

1 tablespoon orange juice

1 tablespoon *nam pla* (Thai fish sauce)

Serves 4

Asian cobb salad
with seven-spice dressing

The traditional cobb salad is a chopped-up mixture of chicken, bacon, hard-boiled eggs, scallions, cheese, and lettuce tossed in a vinaigrette. This updated version is fresh and summery, with a delicious, intriguing dressing of Asian ingredients including the Thai spice mixture called "seven-spice," which includes aromatics such as various chili powders, garlic, ginger, coriander, star anise, cloves, and lemon peel.

Shred the cabbage as finely as possible, and place in a bowl with the shallots, cucumber, carrot, and pear. Heat the sesame oil in a skillet, add the spinach and stir-fry for about 1 minute until green and glistening. Add to the bowl. Mix the dressing ingredients together, then pour over the salad. Sprinkle with sprigs of dill and serve.

8 oz. white cabbage

4 shallots, thinly sliced

½ cucumber, peeled, seeded and finely diced

1 carrot, sliced diagonally

1 pear, sliced

1 tablespoon sesame oil

8 oz. baby spinach leaves

sprigs of dill, to serve

seven-spice dressing

4 tablespoons rice vinegar

1 tablespoon soy sauce

1 garlic clove, crushed

1 tablespoon light sesame oil

2 tablespoons mint leaves, chopped

½ teaspoon Thai seven-spice seasoning

Serves 4

Belgian endive
and fennel with mustard dressing

This crisp, crunchy salad is perfect for winter—and fennel really soaks up the flavors of the dressing. You can change the taste by changing the vinegar—rice vinegar will give a sweet, mild flavor and cider vinegar would be suitable if you used the apple rather than the pear. Belgian endive is juicy and tart, but if you can't find it, radicchio or a small lettuce would be a delicious substitute.

Roughly break the heads of Belgian endive into pieces and arrange on a serving plate. Add the thinly sliced fennel, the watercress or mustard leaves and the sliced pear or apple. To make the mustard dressing, place all the ingredients in a bowl and whisk together. Drizzle over the salad, and sprinkle with the chopped parsley and toasted slivered almonds. Serve with a selection of other salads as an accompaniment to main dishes.

a crunchy, **unusual salad** that looks

very impressive and is very **easy to mak**

4 heads of Belgian
endive (red if available),
or radicchio

1 fennel bulb,
thinly sliced

8 oz. watercress or
mustard leaves

1 pear or 1 crisp apple,
cored and thinly sliced

mustard dressing

4 tablespoons
white wine vinegar

6 tablespoons
virgin olive oil

2 teaspoons
wholegrain mustard

sea salt and freshly
ground black pepper

to serve

1 tablespoon chopped
fresh flat-leaf parsley

1 tablespoon slivered
almonds, toasted

Serves 4

Tuscan panzanella
with tomatoes and capers

A traditional Tuscan salad, based on good
country bread soaked in rich extra-virgin
olive oil and red wine vinegar.

1 loaf of stale
ciabatta bread

1 cup olive oil

2 garlic cloves,
finely mashed

4 tablespoons
red wine vinegar

2 red bell peppers

2 yellow bell peppers

1 lb. ripe red
plum tomatoes

5 tablespoons
capers packed in salt

3 oz. anchovies

½ cup pitted
black olives

1 large bunch of
basil, roughly torn

sea salt and freshly
ground black pepper

Serves 4–6

Roughly chop the bread into thick slices and place in
a large bowl. Mix the olive oil in a small pitcher with
garlic and 2 to 3 tablespoons of the red wine
vinegar, then pour over the bread.
Season with salt and black pepper, and mix well,
adding a little more vinegar if required.
Broil the bell peppers whole until blackened, cover
with plastic wrap for about 5 to 7 minutes, then peel,
seed, and cut into long strips.
Blanch and peel the tomatoes, then cut into quarters.
Place the soaked bread in a serving dish, mix in the
broiled bell peppers, tomatoes, capers, anchovies,
olives, and basil.
Allow to stand for at least 20 minutes and up to
1 hour to develop the flavors, then serve.

Crunchy green salad
with sherry Roquefort dressing

This is a super-simple salad absolutely packed with flavor. Sherry vinegar is marvelous with Roquefort and you can make this combination even more creamy by adding scoops of avocado. Hass, the variety with very dark, bumpy skin, has the best flavor. The croutons are essential for this dish: don't bother cutting them into neat dice—just tear into roughly equal pieces.

To make the croutons, heat the olive oil in a skillet. Add the pieces of torn bread and sauté gently until golden. Drain on paper towels.
To make the dressing, crumble the Roquefort cheese into a bowl, stir in the vinegar, olive oil, sour cream, salt, and freshly ground black pepper, and beat together until creamy.
Break up the lettuces and place in a bowl, sprinkle over the croutons and parsley, then pour over the dressing. Serve as a light appetizer for a summer lunch, or instead of cheese after a main course.

a selection of crisp lettuce leaves, such as romaine, curly endive, or escarole

4 tablespoons torn fresh flat-leaf parsley, to serve

croutons

1 tablespoon extra-virgin olive oil

4 slices sourdough bread, torn into small pieces

Roquefort dressing

1 oz. Roquefort cheese

4 teaspoons sherry vinegar

6 tablespoons olive oil

2 tablespoons sour cream

salt and freshly ground black pepper

Serves 4

a **new twist** on a classic salad—

sherry vinegar gives an extra **dash of flavor**

Appetizers

Marinated tiger shrimp
with lemon and lime

The simplest recipe imaginable—but it looks
and tastes terrific. Cider vinegar gives a
special zing, and marries well with the
lemon, lime, and the fresh taste of cilantro.

Cook the shrimp in a large saucepan of boiling
salted water for a few minutes until they turn pink.
Drain and place in a bowl. Pour over the vinegar and
lime juice, and add the remaining ingredients.
Chill for 2 hours or overnight. Serve with the lime,
lemon, and toasted brîôche.

2 lb. uncooked
tiger shrimp

¾ cup cider vinegar

juice of 2 limes

4 scallions,
roughly chopped

1 tablespoon torn
fresh cilantro leaves

2 red onions,
finely sliced

salt and freshly
ground black pepper

to serve

1 lemon,
cut into wedges

1 lime,
cut into wedges

toasted brîôche bread

Serves 4

Chilled tomato cups
with balsamic vinegar

Whenever you serve tomatoes, make sure
they're as ripe as possible. Aim for vine-
ripened ones, grown in sunny climates, and
choose varieties known for their flavor, such
as the French *Marmande* varieties, and some
of the Italian plum tomatoes, such as *Roma*.
Little cherry tomatoes seem to have more
flavor too. Balsamic vinegar makes the
perfect partner for tomatoes—you might like
to try the quick and easy recipe on page 55.

Cut the tomatoes into quarters, and place in a bowl.
Add the scallions and chives, then sprinkle with
balsamic vinegar, salt, and freshly ground pepper.
Chill for a few hours or overnight.
Spoon the mixture into individual, chilled cups, and
serve, accompanied by toasted country breads.

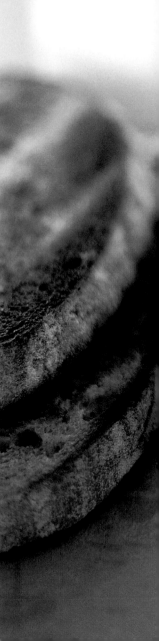

2 lb. ripe tomatoes,
blanched, peeled,
and seeded

2 scallions,
finely chopped

2 tablespoons
snipped fresh chives

4 tablespoons
balsamic vinegar

salt and freshly
ground black pepper

Serves 4

Icy gazpacho
with tarragon vinegar

Tarragon vinegar adds extra herb flavor to gazpacho—the quintessential summer soup, full of the flavor and the color of the sun. The recipe hails from Andalusia, in southern Spain, where the summers can get searingly hot. A gazpacho is quite a substantial soup, and is even filling enough to serve for lunch with crusty country bread.

Roughly chop the tomatoes, green bell pepper, and cucumber, and place in a bowl. Place all the remaining ingredients in a blender or food processor, puree until smooth, then add to the vegetables and chill for a few hours. Spoon into soup bowls and serve with ice cubes and sprigs of basil.

1½ lb. ripe tomatoes, blanched, peeled, seeded, and quartered

1 green bell pepper, cored and seeded

1 large cucumber, peeled and seeded

1 celery stalk, chopped

6 basil leaves, roughly chopped

⅔ cup tomato juice

2–3 tablespoons tarragon vinegar

3 garlic cloves

2 small jalapeño chiles

2 slices white bread, crusts removed

to serve

ice cubes

4–8 sprigs of basil

Serves 4

mild **tarragon** vinegar gives extra zip to

this **classic summer soup**

Crab cakes
with chile mango vinaigrette

Use the freshest crabmeat you can find—
preferably from a crab you've cooked
yourself. However some species can be
tricky to prepare, so it's worth becoming
very friendly with the people at your local
fish market and getting them to do it for you.

Pick over the crabmeat and remove any bits of shell.
Finely chop the bacon, shallots, and celery.
Peel, seed, and finely chop the green bell pepper.
Sauté the bacon in a non-stick skillet for about
2 minutes until lightly browned. Add the shallots,
bell pepper, celery, and garlic, and cook until soft.
Transfer to a bowl and cool.
Stir in the crabmeat, herbs, and seasoning.
Using your hands, shape the mixture into 8 small, flat
patties (the mixture will be quite crumbly).
Wrap in wax paper and chill for at least 30 minutes.
To make the vinaigrette, mix the mango and chile
together, then stir in the vinegar and set aside.
To cook the crab cakes, heat the clarified butter in a
skillet and cook the crab cakes on each side until
golden. Drain and serve immediately with the
vinaigrette and sprigs of cilantro or a salad of
crisp curly endive.

1 lb. white crabmeat

2 shallots

1 celery stalk

1 green bell pepper

2 slices of bacon

1 garlic clove, crushed

2 tablespoons chopped
fresh flat-leaf parsley

2 tablespoons chopped
fresh basil leaves

salt and freshly
ground black pepper

clarified butter,
for frying

sprigs of cilantro, or
curly endive salad,
to serve

chile mango vinaigrette

1 mango, peeled
and roughly chopped

1 red chile,
finely chopped

3–4 tablespoons
sherry vinegar

Serves 4

Entrees

Seared tuna niçoise
with balsamic tomatoes

Serve this colorful dish on a base of steamed couscous, mixed green salad leaves, or mouthwatering Lebanese tabbouleh (parsley, buckwheat, tomatoes, and lemon juice).

Place the tomatoes, onions, black olives, and green beans in a bowl and sprinkle over the balsamic vinegar, salt and freshly ground black pepper. Set aside to marinate while you cook the fish. Mix the crushed garlic and thyme leaves with salt and pepper, and brush over the tuna. Brush a stove-top grill pan or barbecue grill with about 1 tablespoon of the olive oil and heat until hot. Add the tuna and sear well on both sides. Remove from the heat and break the fish into pieces. Add to the bowl of marinated vegetables, pour in the remaining olive oil and mix carefully. To serve, arrange the couscous on a serving plate, then place the tuna salad on top.

3 plum tomatoes, cut into wedges

2 red onions, sliced

4 black olives, such as *olives de provence*

8 oz. green beans, blanched

2 tablespoons balsamic vinegar

3 garlic cloves, crushed

leaves from 3–4 sprigs of lemon thyme

4 tuna steaks, about 4 oz. each

½ cup olive oil

salt and freshly ground black pepper

steamed couscous, to serve

Serves 4

Roast monkfish
with garlic and caperberries

Roasting a big fish fast and furiously seals in all the flavor and juices. The vinegar is used both as a cooking medium and as flavoring. Caperberries, about the size of a small olive, are the fruit of the caper plant. If you can't find them at the market, capers—which are the bud of the plant—may be substituted.

Place the fish in a roasting pan, add the shallots, garlic, thyme, salt, and caperberries or capers, pour over the cider vinegar, and roast in a preheated oven at 400°F for 20 minutes. Place the fish on a serving dish and keep warm. Place the pan on top of the stove and continue cooking until the shallots are cooked and caramelized. Add to the serving dish. Meanwhile, cook the potatoes in boiling salted water for 20 minutes or until tender. Drain and mash. Stir in the olive oil and garlic, then beat in the milk. Serve immediately with the roasted monkfish.

2 lb. monkfish or pompano, filleted

8 oz. shallots, unpeeled

2 garlic cloves

6 sprigs of thyme

½ cup caperberries or capers (preferably packed in salt)

⅔ cup cider vinegar

1 tablespoon sea salt

garlic mash

1 lb. potatoes

5 tablespoons virgin olive oil

1 garlic clove, crushed

4 tablespoons milk

Serves 4

cider vinegar gives **a sweet, sharp**

edge to an **easy but spectacular** recipe

Marinated roast lamb
with Moroccan stuffing

Cooking meat and fruit together is typical
of the great Arab cuisines of North Africa
and the Middle East—and also of medieval
European and Elizabethan cooking.

To make the stuffing, place the pignoli nuts in the
oven or in a skillet and toast until golden (do not
burn). Mix in the remaining stuffing ingredients.
Place the boned lamb on a chopping board and
open out the meat. Spoon the stuffing along the
center where the bone used to be, then roll up, and
tie with string. Place in a deep dish, pour over the oil
and vinegar, and season with salt and pepper.
Marinate in the refrigerator for 2 hours, or up to
2 days. Remove 1 hour before cooking.
When ready to cook, remove from the marinade and
place in a roasting pan. Tuck the rosemary and garlic
under the meat. Pour over 3 tablespoons of
marinade and roast in a preheated oven at 400°F,
allowing 20 minutes per pound, plus 20 minutes
extra, to produce pink lamb (longer if you prefer well-
done meat.) Baste with the juices from time to time.
Remove the meat from the pan and set aside to rest
in a warm place. Pour off all but 2 tablespoons of
juice from the roasting pan and stir in the flour.
Cook gently for 1 minute, then stir in the stock and
cook, stirring, until the gravy has thickened.
Carve the lamb and serve, accompanied by seasonal
vegetables or a spiced Moroccan couscous.

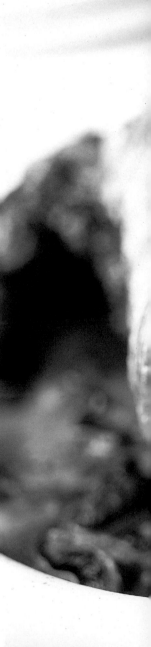

1 leg of lamb,
butterfly boned

2 tablespoons olive oil

⅔ cup red wine vinegar

2 sprigs of rosemary

2 garlic cloves, sliced

1 tablespoon flour

1½ cups
vegetable stock

salt and freshly
ground black pepper

Moroccan stuffing

½ cup pignoli nuts

1½ cups dried apricots,
roughly chopped

4 tablespoons chopped
fresh flat-leaf parsley

2 tablespoons chopped
fresh rosemary leaves

1 tablespoon
balsamic vinegar

salt and freshly
ground black pepper

Serves 4

vinegar, ginger, a

sharp, hot, a

Pork tenderloin
with mango and ginger sauce

Rich sherry vinegar gives this mango and ginger sauce the kind of sharpness that's especially suited to pork.

To make the marinade, mix the sherry vinegar, soy sauce, sesame oil, and orange juice together. Place the pork in a roasting pan, pour over the marinade, and set aside for 30 minutes. To make the sauce, peel and dice the mangoes, seed and dice the chile, and mince the ginger. Place all the ingredients in a saucepan, bring to a boil, then simmer for 15 minutes. Pass through a strainer to give a smooth consistency. Place the roasting pan containing the pork and its marinade in a preheated oven and roast at 400°F for about 20 to 30 minutes. Remove from the oven and set aside to keep warm for 5 to 10 minutes to allow the meat to rest. Steamed green beans or noodles tossed together with sesame oil and sesame seeds would be suitable accompaniments.

1 lb. pork fillet

sesame marinade

2 tablespoons sherry vinegar

2 tablespoons soy sauce

1 tablespoon sesame oil

juice of ½ orange

salt and freshly ground black pepper

mango and ginger sauce

2 mangoes

1 serrano chile

1-inch piece of fresh ginger

1 tablespoon light brown sugar

2 tablespoons sherry vinegar

salt and freshly ground black pepper

Serves 4

angoes produce

veet tastes—all great with pork

Pork spareribs
with tamarind sauce

A sweet-sour recipe from Thailand which works equally well with pork spareribs or free-range chicken wings. Tomatoes and brown sugar provide the sweet tastes, while tamarind and rice vinegar produce the sour.

To make the sauce, place the sun-dried tomatoes in a bowl, pour over boiling water, soak for 20 minutes, then chop roughly.
Blanch, peel and chop the plum tomatoes.
Heat a large skillet until very hot, then add the oil and plum tomatoes, and cook until browned.
Place in a food processor with the sun-dried tomatoes and puree until smooth.
Return the mixture to a saucepan, then add all the remaining sauce ingredients. Set aside while you prepare the spareribs.
Peel and slice the ginger, and place in a saucepan with the ribs. Pour over the rice wine, bring to a boil, and simmer for about 10 to 15 minutes. Drain the ribs, and reheat the tomato and tamarind sauce.
Serve the ribs with the sauce poured over, accompanied by steamed fragrant Thai rice, or cellophane noodles sprinkled with freshly toasted cashew nuts.

1-inch piece of fresh ginger

1 lb. pork spareribs, free-range if possible

1 cup rice wine

tamarind sauce

3 sun-dried tomatoes

3 ripe plum tomatoes

2 teaspoons sunflower oil

1 tablespoon tamarind puree

2 tablespoons hoisin sauce

¼ cup rice vinegar

2 tablespoons brown sugar

1 garlic clove, crushed

1-inch piece of fresh ginger, minced

1 bunch of scallions, sliced diagonally

to serve

fragrant Thai rice, or cellophane noodles

toasted cashew nuts

Serves 4

Stir-fried chicken
in a sherry vinegar marinade

An easy, modern update of a Chinese
classic—and you don't have to be a pro
with the cleaver or chopsticks!

To prepare the marinade, whisk the egg white with
the sherry vinegar, cornstarch, sugar, and salt. Slice
the chicken breasts into strips, add to the marinade,
then chill for about 20 minutes.
Place the sauce ingredients in a saucepan, bring to a
boil, then simmer for about 7 minutes. Set aside.
Heat the oil in a large skillet or wok, then add the
scallions, garlic, and ginger, and stir-fry quickly.
Using a slotted spoon, remove the chicken strips
from the marinade and add to the hot oil.
Stir-fry quickly for about 5 to 7 minutes until tender.
Add the snow peas and spinach, and stir-fry quickly.
Prepare the noodles according to the package
instructions. To serve, reheat the sauce, place the
noodles on heated plates, add the stir-fried
chicken mixture, and pour over the sauce.

a ne

with sher

...pproach to the classic Chinese stir-fry—

...negar giving **extra depth** to the marinade

4 boneless
chicken breasts

1 tablespoon
sunflower oil

4 scallions, sliced

1 garlic clove, crushed

2-inch piece of
fresh ginger, grated

8 oz. snow peas

8 oz. spinach

12 oz. egg noodles

marinade

1 egg white

1 tablespoon
sherry vinegar

1 tablespoon
cornstarch

1 teaspoon sugar

1 teaspoon salt

sherry sauce

4 tablespoons
chicken stock

1 tablespoon sherry

1 tablespoon
rice vinegar

Serves 4

Entrees **39**

Seared duck breasts
with gingered sweet potato

Rich sherry vinegar is used to deglaze
the skillet and to enhance the flavors of
scallions and chile oil.

2 large duck breasts

2 tablespoons
soy sauce

1 tablespoon chile oil

6 scallions

2 tablespoons
sherry vinegar

⅔ cup chicken stock

**gingered sweet
potato mash**

1 lb. sweet potatoes

1-inch piece of
fresh ginger, minced

1 tablespoon
unsalted butter

Serves 4

To make the mash, cook the sweet potatoes in
boiling salted water until tender, then mash with the
minced ginger. Add the butter and beat in well with a
wooden spoon. Keep warm until ready to serve.

To prepare the duck, cut the breasts into three
pieces, score the skin in a criss-cross pattern and
brush with the soy sauce. Heat the chile oil in a
stove-top grill pan or skillet until very hot, then add
the duck, skin side down, and sear for a few minutes.
Cut the scallions into large chunks and add to the
skillet. Turn the duck over and sear the other side,
searing the scallions at the same time.
Remove the duck from the skillet and keep warm.
Add the vinegar to deglaze the skillet, simmer for a
few minutes, then add the stock, bring to a boil and
simmer until reduced by half.
To serve, place the sweet potato mash on heated
plates, slice the duck breasts, and place on top of
the mash, with the sauce drizzled over.

Grains and beans

Wild rice salad
with ginger balsamic vinaigrette

Wild rice isn't a rice at all, but a grass native to North America. It looks wonderful on its own or mixed with other rice (though you should cook them separately, because wild rice takes much longer to cook than ordinary rice). It seems to have a more interesting taste as well, and is terrific in salads where it can be treated as the main ingredient.

Wash the rice several times in cold water, until the water runs clear. Place the rice in a saucepan with salted water to cover, bring to a slow boil over a gentle heat and simmer, uncovered, for 20 minutes. Turn off the heat and allow to stand for 10 minutes. Meanwhile, mix the vinaigrette dressing ingredients together. Drain the rice and pour the dressing over the salad. Stir in the bell peppers and scallions, then serve immediately with green salad leaves, if using.

1 cup wild rice

1 yellow bell pepper, cored, seeded, and sliced

1 bunch of scallions, sliced

salad leaves, to serve (optional)

ginger balsamic vinaigrette

6 tablespoons sunflower oil

1 tablespoon chile oil

1-inch piece of fresh ginger, minced

1 tablespoon balsamic vinegar

2 teaspoons lemon juice

Serves 4

Warm white beans
with thyme and tomatoes

Add the dressing to the beans while they're
still warm, so they absorb lots of flavor.
Cannellinis are smooth and creamy, and
delicious with the extra sharpness of this
herb vinaigrette. Don't add salt to the beans
until halfway through the cooking time—
otherwise they'll take forever to cook.

Cover the beans with cold water, and soak for at
least 2 hours (or overnight).
Drain, place in a saucepan with the onion and celery,
cover with fresh water, bring to a boil, lower the heat,
and cook gently for 30 minutes.
Add salt, and continue cooking for another
30 minutes or until just tender.
Drain the beans and place in a bowl.
Place the vinegar, olive oil, garlic, and thyme in a
saucepan and heat gently.
Add the beans and simmer for 10 minutes, then stir
in the tomato and cucumber to warm through.
Serve, sprinkled with the roughly torn parsley.

1 cup dried
cannellini beans

1 onion,
roughly chopped

2 celery stalks,
chopped

4 tablespoons
white wine vinegar

2 tablespoons
virgin olive oil

2 garlic cloves, crushed

3 sprigs of thyme

2 ripe plum tomatoes,
halved, seeded
and chopped

½ cucumber, peeled,
seeded and sliced

salt and freshly
ground black pepper

4 tablespoons roughly
torn flat-leaf parsley,
to serve

Serves 4

great for a **winter lunch**—

and **splendid fare** for vegetarians

Buckwheat noodles
with sesame and sugar snap peas

Noodles are great, hot or cold, and make a good base for salads instead of that eighties eternal—the dreaded pasta salad!

Cook the buckwheat noodles in boiling water for about 2 minutes, or according to the package instructions, then drain.
Blanch the sugar snap peas in boiling salted water for about 1 minute. Drain, run under cold running water, then drain again.
To make the dressing, pour the soy sauce into a saucepan, bring to a boil over a high heat, and reduce by half. Remove from the heat, add the remaining dressing ingredients, stir until the sugar dissolves, then add the peas.
Mix the noodles into the dressing and serve, sprinkled with sesame seeds.

8 oz. buckwheat noodles

4 oz. sugar snap peas

1 cucumber, peeled, halved, seeded, and thickly sliced diagonally into half moons

1 tablespoon sesame seeds, to serve

sesame dressing

⅔ cup soy sauce

1 teaspoon superfine sugar

2 tablespoons sesame oil

4 tablespoons chile oil

3 tablespoons balsamic vinegar

6 scallions, thinly sliced diagonally

Serves 4

noodles make **great salads** a

vinegar and sesame oil a

lsamic

licious companions

Vegetables

Leek vinaigrette
with soft boiled egg and anchovies

The salty taste of anchovies combines well with soft egg and crisp, sweetly flavored leeks. Tiny baguette leeks really make this recipe special—and an ideal vegetarian appetizer—but if you can't find baguettes, just use the thinnest leeks available.

Trim the the roots off the leeks, then cut off all but the last 1 to 2 inches of green. Using a knife, split the ends from halfway along the white to the end of the green part. Rinse thoroughly under running water to wash out all the sand. If using large leeks, cut into 3-inch lengths. Cook in a saucepan of boiling salted water for about 5 minutes until tender. Drain thoroughly, and squeeze out any excess water. To soft-boil the egg, place it in cold water, bring to a boil, then simmer (taking 5 minutes from cold). Plunge it into cold water to stop the cooking process, then peel and roughly chop. To make the dressing, place the shallot in a bowl, whisk in the vinegar, olive oil, and parsley, and season with salt and black pepper. Stir the leeks into the dressing, add the egg and anchovies, then serve with toasted sourdough bread.

2 bunches of baguette leeks, or 3 young leeks

1 egg

6 anchovies

toasted sourdough bread, to serve

vinaigrette

1 shallot, finely diced

3 tablespoons white wine vinegar

4 tablespoons virgin olive oil

1 tablespoon chopped fresh flat-leaf parsley

salt and freshly ground black pepper

Serves 4

Seared eggplant
with lemongrass vinaigrette

Buy lemongrass-flavored rice vinegar ready
made, or make your own by bruising 2 stalks
of lemongrass, then steeping in a bottle of
rice vinegar for about 2 weeks. If available,
use Japanese eggplant, which are small and
round, but other varieties can also be used.

Mix the dressing ingredients together and set aside.
Brush the eggplant slices with chile oil, then sear on
a stove-top grill pan or skillet for 3 to 5 minutes until
tender. Alternatively, cook under a very hot broiler.
Cut into wedges and place in a bowl with the roasted
red bell pepper and seasoning. Pour over the
dressing and serve.

4 Japanese eggplants, unpeeled, sliced lengthwise (or 1 large one, halved and thickly sliced

chile oil, for brushing

1 red bell pepper, roasted, peeled, seeded, and cut into thick pieces

salt and freshly ground black pepper

chile-lemongrass vinaigrette

4 tablespoons lemongrass-flavored rice vinegar (see the recipe introduction opposite)

1 teaspoon soy sauce

a pinch of sugar

1–2 tablespoons chile oil

1 garlic clove, crushed

2 tablespoons roughly chopped cilantro leaves

Serves 4

lemongrass vinegar mixed with

chile oil gives a great Southeast Asian flavor

Summer tian
with baby eggplant

Tians are Provençal vegetable gratins, baked in a shallow earthenware roasting dish called a tian. If you roast the vegetables separately first for about 10 minutes, the flavor of this traditional recipe becomes even more interesting. If you can't find Japanese eggplants, use ordinary ones cut in half lengthwise, then thickly sliced.

6 plum tomatoes, thickly sliced

1 red onion, sliced

4 Japanese eggplants, unpeeled, halved lengthwise

4 small zucchini, sliced lengthwise

5 tablespoons virgin olive oil

2 tablespoons herb vinegar

2 garlic cloves, crushed

2 teaspoons fresh thyme leaves

salt and pepper

Serves 4

Brush all the vegetables with 1 tablespoon of the olive oil and roast in a preheated oven at 400°F for about 10 minutes.
Mix the remaining olive oil in a bowl with the vinegar, garlic, thyme, salt, and pepper.
Transfer the vegetables to the bowl, and toss until well coated with the dressing.
Layer the vegetables in a gratin dish, cover with aluminum foil, return to the oven, and cook at 400°F for about 25 minutes. Remove the foil and cook for another 15 minutes.
Serve hot with country bread drizzled with olive oil.

Baby zucchini
in a hot mustard vinaigrette

1 tablespoon mustard
seeds, crushed

⅔ cup red wine vinegar

1 lb. baby zucchini

1 red onion, sliced

Serves 4

This is an unexpected way to prepare sweet
tasting baby zucchini—the mustard seeds
give the dish an interesting crunch and kick.

Gently heat the mustard seeds and vinegar together
in a small saucepan. Remove from the heat.
Peel the zucchini in strips, and cut into 1½-inch
pieces if large.
Bring a saucepan of salted water to a boil, add the
zucchini, and blanch for 1 minute. Drain, place in a
bowl, and add the sliced onion.
Pour over the mustard vinegar and serve with meat
dishes, or with salami as an antipasto.

Vine-ripened tomatoes
with balsamic vinegar

1 lb. vine-ripened
cherry tomatoes

2–3 tablespoons
balsamic vinegar

freshly ground
black pepper

4 basil leaves, torn

pinch of sugar

Serves 4

A very simple but amazing dish—balsamic
vinegar marries perfectly with tomatoes.

Cut the tomatoes into quarters, place in a
bowl, sprinkle with the remaining ingredients,
and serve with suitable accompaniments, such
as arugula leaves, field lettuce or lamb's
lettuce, and Italian mozzarella or other cheese.

Pickles

Pickled vegetables
with chile rice vinegar

Mild and slightly sweet, rice vinegar gives these vegetables a wonderfully mellow flavor. But you could substitute other vinegars—obviously each type will give a different taste. Rice vinegar is widely used in Chinese and Japanese cooking—and this pickle would also be a crunchy addition to a Thai noodle salad, mixed with shredded chicken or mixed seafood.

To blanch the carrots and beans, plunge them into boiling water for 1 minute. Drain, then quickly run under cold water to halt the cooking process. Drain again and place in a bowl. Pour over the rice vinegar, salt, and sugar, then add the onion and chile. Spoon into a clean, sterilized glass jar. Refrigerate for several days to allow the flavors to develop. Serve with accompaniments such as a selection of cold meats, serrano ham, salami, and lots of fresh, crusty country bread.

1 bunch of baby carrots

8 oz. green beans

1 cup rice vinegar

½ teaspoon sugar

1 large white onion, finely sliced

1 serrano chile, cored, seeded, and finely sliced

sea salt, to taste

Serves 4

Pickled ginger

You can buy pickled ginger in Asian grocers, but homemade is much nicer—and it's easy!

Peel the ginger with a vegetable peeler and slice it very thinly. Blanch in boiling water for 20 seconds, then drain. Place in a bowl, sprinkle with salt, and set aside for 30 minutes. Pour off any liquid that accumulates. Combine the vinegar and sugar, pour over the ginger and toss well. Spoon into a sterilized jar and refrigerate for up to 1 week before using.

1 lb. fresh ginger

1 tablespoon salt

2 tablespoons rice vinegar

4 tablespoons sugar

Makes one 1-pint jar

Pickled shallots

Shallots are easy to grow in the garden—and once you plant them, you'll have millions! This is a marvelous way to use them up.

To peel the shallots, place in a bowl, pour over boiling water (this will reduce their pungent aroma), then slip off the skins and discard. Mix the sugar, salt, water, and vinegar in a pan, and bring to a boil. Wash three ½-pint glass jars thoroughly, then place in a large pan, cover with water, bring slowly to a boil, then drain. Pack the jars with the shallots and pour in the boiling vinegar. Seal the jars and loosely fit the lids. Process in a boiling water bath for 10 minutes, then let cool, tighten the seals, and store in the refrigerator.*

1 lb. shallots

2 tablespoons brown sugar

1 tablespoon sea salt

1 cup water

1 cup herb vinegar

Makes three ½-pint jars

*Pickles should be processed in a boiling water-bath canner according to USDA guidelines.

Cranberry jelly
with chiles and bell pepper

Cranberry juice makes a delicious jelly.

Place the chiles, bell pepper, and half the vinegar in a bowl, and set aside. Pour the cranberry juice into a saucepan, stir in the sugar, and cook over a medium heat, stirring until the sugar is dissolved. Skim off any foam. Stir in the chile mixture, then the remaining vinegar. (Add more vinegar for a sharper flavor.) Boil over a medium heat for 6 to 8 minutes until syrupy. Continue to skim. Add the pectin, boil for 3 minutes, and skim if required. Pour into a large, sterilized Mason jar and seal tightly. Cool at room temperature, then refrigerate. Use within 1 month.

1–2 Scotch bonnet or habanero chiles, seeded and finely chopped

¼ yellow bell pepper, seeded and finely chopped

1 cup red wine vinegar

2½ cups cranberry juice

2 cups white sugar

5 tablespoons liquid pectin

Makes one 1-quart jar

Papaya relish

A simple, fresh, Asian-style relish—great with cold meats, sausages, and salads.

Peel the papayas, cut in half, scoop out the seeds, and dice the flesh. Slice the bell peppers and onion. Place in a bowl with the remaining ingredients, stir well, and chill for 1 to 2 hours, stirring several times. Serve with cold meats.

2 medium papayas

1 red bell pepper

1 red onion

2 tablespoons torn fresh cilantro leaves

1 tablespoon lime juice

⅔ cup red wine vinegar

1 teaspoon honey

pinch of salt

Serves 4

Below, from left, Pickled ginger (recipe page 58), Papaya relish (page 59), Pickled shallots (page 58), and Cranberry jelly (page 59).

Traditional fruitcake

Vinegar is a totally unexpected ingredient in cake making—but it produces a lighter result than eggs, because the baking soda and vinegar act as the rising agents.

Grease a deep, round, 9-inch cake pan. Mix the butter into the flour until the mixture resembles fine breadcrumbs, then stir in the fruit and sugar. Sprinkle the baking soda into the milk, then stir in the vinegar. The mixture will foam after about 2 minutes. While still frothing, add to the dry ingredients and mix well. Spoon into the prepared cake pan and bake in a preheated oven at 400°F for 30 minutes. Reduce to 325°F and cook for 1½ hours until firm to the touch. If the top becomes too brown, cover with parchment. Cool in the pan for 30 minutes, then turn out onto a wire rack, and cool completely.

1 cup butter

4 cups plain flour

2⅔ cups mixed dried fruit

2 cups firmly packed light brown sugar

1 teaspoon baking soda

1¼ cups milk

3 tablespoons malt vinegar

Makes one 9-inch cake

a **totally unexpected** use for vinegar—

a cake with a crunchy **sweet crust**

Index